Brely Evans

presents

The ABCs of I AMs

A DAILY GUIDE FOR SPEAKING PROSPERITY,
LOVE AND SUCCESS INTO YOUR LIFE

Brely Evans

ISBN: 978-1-7361763-0-6 (Hardback)
          978-1-7361763-2-0 (Paperback)
          978-1-7361763-1-3 (E-book)

Library of Congress Control Number: 2020922942

Front cover image by Water Walkers Worldwide, Inc.
Book design by Water Walkers Worldwide, Inc.

Printed by Water Walkers Worldwide in the United States of America.

First printing edition 2020.

Water Walkers Worldwide, Inc
2711 N Sepulveda Blvd #443
Manhattan Beach, CA 90266

www.BrelyEvans.com

Acknowledgements

I've come to realize that nothing I do is a complete origination from myself, but it's a collective of experiences and my loved ones who are all around me. I'd like to acknowledge a few people for this first offering that I give of my ink to paper.

Mom and Dad, thank you for giving me life and one that has been plentiful and beautiful. Granny, my Angel, Etta Yarborough, thank you for introducing me to our Lord and Savior, Jesus Christ. Thank you to every friend and fan who has supported me over the years.

Special thanks to my girlfriends: Christina Johnson, for inspiring me to stay *Quenched in my Quest for Life*; Thank you to, Tabitha Brown for inspiring me to do things well so that I can say they are *Very Good* at the end; Thank you to my cousin, Stacy Hogg, for reminding me daily that I am *Unstoppable in the face of No Agreement*; Amesha Mason, thank you, because it was at your house that I had refuge and God spoke to me to put this book together. It was at your desk that I was able to hear from heaven the words that everyone will read in this book. I love you sister-friend. These are just a few words that will show up in this book that I gleaned from the people I love.

I also would like to give a special thanks to those who contributed words in the X, Y and Z, Raesaundra Lightner. My Instagram family, you guys have pushed me to this moment and I just can't stop thanking you, I thank you so much. Thank you to Thembisa Mshaka for believing in me and being my eyes on this book. I would be remised if I did not thank, Marcus Jackson and Tiffany Thomas, all I have is two words for yall, Dream Team. Now let's speak and change lives all over the world.

Writing books doesn't have a purpose unless people read them and buy them. So, I have to acknowledge my family at Rolling Out, Munson Steed, for being the first to purchase. Now if I have left anyone out, please charge it to my mind and to the two years that it has taken to get this book out. I love you and I honor you all.

Thank you!

I

Introduction

CREATE THE DAY BEFORE YOU EVEN BEGIN

Brely Evans presents The ABCs of I AMs so that you can declare from your mouth positive affirmations that will speak to the very depth of your soul on a daily basis. What one declares from his mouth can change the dynamic of any situation and self-perception. You have the choice to speak DEATH or you can speak LIFE... Brely Evans challenges you to speak LIFE by affirming who you are and believing what you have affirmed.

SPEAK WHAT IT IS THAT YOU DESIRE TO SEE!

Note from Brely

If you are holding this book, you are officially a *Water Walker!* What that means is that you are willing to do things that are IMPOSSIBLE to some because when you see those words, you see I'M POSSIBLE.

This tool is to be used right after you get up in the morning and you say thanks for another day. Pick it up and begin in the As and go all the way to Z declaring out loud your I AMs. When you speak out loud, you are moving the molecules in the very room to boomerang back to your life, what you just said. Actually, EVERYTHING you say is boomeranging back to you, that's why you must be careful about what you speak!

But again, make these declarations, as you turn each page, say them out loud with all of the boldness and the confidence you have.

Love Yall,

Prayer

Thank you, Heavenly Father, for this opportunity to speak to your people on your behalf. Sit me down and you stand up. Give your people what they need for this day. Let them declare who they are in you.

Amen.

I AM

"And my God shall supply all your needs according
To His riches in glory by Christ Jesus."
Philippians 4:19 (NKJV)

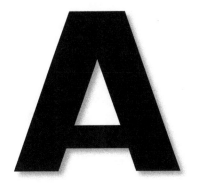

Say It...

I AM ABUNDANT

Being abundant reminds us that we lack
nothing; that EVERYTHING is available
to us. We can move forward without
the fear of not having enough!

I AM _____

_____

_____

_____

_____

_____

_____

_____

_____

_____

_____

_____

_____

_____

_____

_____

I AM

"So, God created human beings [a] in His
own image. In the image of God,
He created them; male and female He created them."
Genesis 1:27 (NLT)

I AM AMAZING

Being amazing reflects your talents, your personality and what you bring to the world when you wake up every day! Let's face it. YOU are amazing!

I AM _____

_____

_____

_____

_____

_____

_____

_____

_____

_____

_____

_____

_____

_____

_____

_____

_____

I AM

"Then you shall take the anointing oil and pour it on his head and anoint him."

Exodus 29:7 (NASB)

I AM ANOINTED

Being anointed means we accept the God given charge that has been placed on our life, understanding that it's meaningful and powerful!

I AM _____

_____

_____

_____

_____

_____

_____

_____

_____

_____

_____

_____

_____

_____

_____

_____

_____

I AM

"Am I now trying to win the favor and
approval of men, or of God?
Or am I seeking to please someone? If I were still trying to be
popular with men, I would not be a bond-servant of Christ."
Galatians 1:10 (AMP)

I AM APPROVED

Being approved is the confidence in Christ validated, and the acceptance of God's mandate on your life – you do not need the approval of man.

I AM _____

_____

_____

_____

_____

_____

_____

_____

_____

_____

_____

_____

_____

_____

_____

_____

_____

_____

I AM

"And I give them eternal life, and they shall never perish; neither shall anyone snatch them out of My hand."

John 10:28 (NKJV)

Say It...

I AM ACCEPTED

Being accepted into the Body of Christ,
means you can never be plucked out!

I AM _____

_____

_____

_____

_____

_____

_____

_____

_____

_____

_____

_____

_____

_____

_____

_____

_____

I AM

"Therefore, if anyone is in Christ, he is a new creation; old things have Passed away; behold, all things have become new."
II Corinthians 5:17 (NKJV)

"Jesus said to him, "I am the way, the truth, and the life. No one comes to The Father except through Me."
John 14:6 (NKJV)

Say It...

I AM BELIEVER

Being a believer is declaring that Jesus
Christ is Lord – and believing He died
on the cross and rose on the third
day with all power in His hands.

I AM _____

_____

_____

_____

_____

_____

_____

_____

_____

_____

_____

_____

_____

_____

_____

_____

I AM

"Let us therefore come boldly to the throne of grace, that we may obtain mercy and find grace to help him in time of need."
Hebrews 4:16 (NKJV)

"Now this is the confidence that we have in Him, that if we ask anything according to His will, He hears us. And if we know that He hears us, whatever we ask, we know that we have the petitions that we have asked of Him."
1 John 5:14-15 (NKJV)

Say It...

I AM BOLD

Being bold is having a knowing that things
will work; a knowing so strong, that you
move forward in the absence of clarity.

I AM _____

_____

_____

_____

_____

_____

_____

_____

_____

_____

_____

_____

_____

_____

_____

_____

I AM

"But He said, "On the contrary, blessed
[happy, favored by God] are those
Who hear the word of God and continually observe it."
Luke 11:28 (AMP)

"Blessed [happy, spiritually prosperous, favored by God]
is the man who is steadfast under trial and perseveres
when tempted; for when he has passed the test and been
approved, he will receive the [victor's] crown of life
which the Lord has promised to those who love Him."
James 1:12 (AMP)

Say It...

I AM BLESSED

Being blessed is having the ability to access resources, opportunities and knowledge given to you freely. Every breath you take proves that you are BLESSED!

I AM _____

_____

_____

_____

_____

_____

_____

_____

_____

_____

_____

_____

_____

_____

_____

_____

_____

I AM

"He has made everything beautiful and appropriate in its time. He has also planted eternity [a sense of divine purpose] in the human heart [a mysterious longing which nothing under the sun can satisfy, except God] – yet man cannot find out [comprehend, grasp] what God has done [His overall plan] from the beginning to the end."

Ecclesiastes 3:11 (AMP)

I AM BALANCED

Being balanced allows you to do
multiple things: everything will be
attended to... just in its own time.

I AM _____

_____

_____

_____

_____

_____

_____

_____

_____

_____

_____

_____

_____

_____

_____

_____

_____

_____

I AM

"And we know [with great confidence] that God [who is deeply concerned about us] causes all things to work together [as a plan] for good for those who love God, to those who are called according to His plan and purpose."
Romans 8:28 (AMP)

"He will not fear bad news; His heart is steadfast, trusting [confidently relying on and believing] in the Lord."
Psalms 112:7 (AMP)

I AM BRAVE

Being brave is having the courage to take risks. Without risks, there is no real success! Having faith requires bravery. The answers are not always right in front of you. They are sometimes hidden on the other side of fear, so you must walk through the things that you fear to get the good stuff!

I AM _____

_____

_____

_____

_____

_____

_____

_____

_____

_____

_____

_____

_____

_____

_____

I AM

"The earth was without form, and void; and darkness
was on the face of the deep. And the Spirit of God
was hovering over the face of the waters."
Genesis 1:2 (NKJV)

"For we are His workmanship, created
in Christ Jesus for good works,
which God prepared beforehand that we should walk in them."
Ephesians 2:10 (NKJV)

I AM CREATIVE

With intellect and imagination, you have the ability to create something out of nothing and make Life extraordinary.

I AM _____

_____

_____

_____

_____

_____

_____

_____

_____

_____

_____

_____

_____

_____

_____

_____

_____

I AM

"No weapon formed against you shall prosper, And every
tongue which rises against you in judgment you shall
condemn. This is the heritage of the servants of the Lord,
and their righteousness is from Me, Says the Lord."
Isaiah 54:17 (NKJV)

"And we know that all things work together
for good to those who love God,
to those who are the called according to His purpose."
Romans 8:28 (NKJV)

Say It...

I AM A CONQUEROR

Being a conqueror is being willing to show up to any fight in your life with no guarantee of victory and the best part is, it is written that you're MORE than a conqueror.

I AM _____

_____

_____

_____

_____

_____

_____

_____

_____

_____

_____

_____

_____

_____

_____

_____

_____

I AM

"For where two or three gather in my name, there am I with them."

Matthew 18:20 (NIV)

I AM CONSIDERATE

Being considerate is being mindful
of our families, friendships, and
loved ones; it's acknowledging that
we aren't on this earth alone.

I AM _____

_____

_____

_____

_____

_____

_____

_____

_____

_____

_____

_____

_____

_____

_____

_____

_____

_____

I AM

"I am convinced and confident of this very thing, that He who has begun a good work in you will [continue to] perfect and complete it until the day of Christ Jesus [the time of His return]."
Philippians 1:6 (NIV)

"Study and do your best to present yourself to God approved, a workman [tested by trial] who has no reason to be ashamed, accurately handling and skillfully teaching the word of truth."
2 Timothy 2:15 (AMP)

Say It...

I AM COMPLETE

Being complete within yourself is being self-sustainable in every area. So, when you connect with others, it's two whole individuals joining forces! You cannot offer any parts of yourself to someone from a half-full vessel.

I AM _____

_____

_____

_____

_____

_____

_____

_____

_____

_____

_____

_____

_____

_____

_____

_____

_____

I AM

"Before I formed you in the womb, I knew you [and approved of you as My chosen instrument], And before you were born I consecrated you [to Myself as My own]; I have appointed you as a prophet to the nations."
Jeremiah 1:5 (AMP)

"For many are called [invited, summoned], but few are chosen."
Jeremiah 22:14 (AMP)

Say It...

I AM CHOSEN

Being chosen indicates that there is a serious
and indeed a divine purpose for why your
father's sperm hit your mother's egg!

I AM _____

_____

_____

_____

_____

_____

_____

_____

_____

_____

_____

_____

_____

_____

I AM

"Christ arrives right on time to make this happen. He didn't, and doesn't wait for us to get ready. He presented himself for this sacrificial death when we were far too weak and rebellious to do anything to get ourselves ready. And even if we hadn't been so weak, we wouldn't have known what to do anyway. We can understand someone dying for a person worth dying for, and we can understand how someone good and noble could inspire us to selfless sacrifice. But God put his love on the line for us by offering his Son in sacrificial death while we were of no use whatever to him."

Romans 5:6-8 (MSG)

Say It...

I AM DELIVERED

Being delivered means that I'm a new creature, I don't do the things I use to do, I don't think the way I use to think, and I don't go where I use to go, say what I use to say, I am delivered from my past on my way to a new pathway.

I AM _____

_____

_____

_____

_____

_____

_____

_____

_____

_____

_____

_____

_____

_____

_____

_____

_____

I AM

"So here's what I want to do, God helping you: Take your everyday, ordinary life – your sleeping, eating, going-to-work, and walking-around life – and place it before God as an offering. Embracing what God does for you is the best thing you can do for Him. Don't become so well-adjusted to your culture that you fit into it without even thinking. Instead, fix your attention on God. You'll be changed from the inside out. Readily recognize what he wants from you, and quickly respond to it. Unlike the culture around you, always dragging you down to its level of immaturity, God bring the best out of you, develops well-formed maturity in you."

Romans 12:1-2 (MSG)

Say It...

I AM DIFFERENT

Being different is celebrating the fingerprint that God gave us. He made every individual very special and unique on purpose and that we are to celebrate, expose, and exploit that. Be Different!

I AM _____

_____

_____

_____

_____

_____

_____

_____

_____

_____

_____

_____

_____

_____

_____

_____

I AM

"Keep vigilant watch over your heart; that's where life starts. Don't talk out of both sides of your mouth; avoid careless banter, white lies, and gossip. Keep your eyes straight ahead; ignore all sideshow distractions. Watch your step, and the road will stretch out smooth before you. Look neither right nor left; leave evil in the dust."

Proverbs 4:23-27(MSG)

I AM DISCIPLINED

Being disciplined means to have a routine that you do regularly every day. My discipline is to wake up, pray, meditate, and speak my I AMs and this discipline helps me have a more productive day every day. It allows me to live a better life each day and the days I don't do it, I notice it.

I AM _____

_____

_____

_____

_____

_____

_____

_____

_____

_____

_____

_____

_____

I AM

"I, Jude, am a slave to Jesus Christ and brother to James, writing to those loved by God the Father, called and kept safe by Jesus Christ. Relax, everything's going to be all right; rest, everything's coming together; open your hearts, love is on the way!"

Jude 1:1-2 (MSG)

Say It...

I AM DESIRABLE

Being desirable is knowing that you have
something to offer to someone that is amazing.
You have love to give, you can be desired by
another person, and you have what it takes
to be in a loving and caring relationship.

I AM _____

_____

_____

_____

_____

_____

_____

_____

_____

_____

_____

_____

_____

_____

_____

_____

I AM

"Then Jesus turned to the Jews who had claimed to believe in him. "If you stick with this, living out what I tell you, you are my disciples for sure. Then you will experience for yourselves the truth, and the truth will free you."
John 8:31-32 (MSG)

Say It...

I AM DRIVEN

Being driven means to put your foot on the gas, and the passion inside of you is driving you to succeed, driving you to doing what's necessary to get your goals accomplished.

I AM _____

_____

_____

_____

_____

_____

_____

_____

_____

_____

_____

_____

_____

_____

_____

_____

_____

"Your word is a lamp to my feet And a light to my path."
Psalm 119:105 (AMP)

"But the fruit of the Spirit is love, joy, peace, long-suffering, kindness, goodness, faithfulness, meekness, temperance, against such there is no law."
Galatians 5:22-23 (NKJV)

Say It...

I AM EQUIPPED

Being equipped means, realizing you have EVERYTHING you need inside of you to be successful. What you have within is enough.

I AM _____

_____

_____

_____

_____

_____

_____

_____

_____

_____

_____

_____

_____

_____

_____

_____

_____

_____

I AM

"And the LORD God formed man of the dust of the ground, and breathed into his nostrils the breath of life; and man became a living being."
Genesis 2:7 (NKJV)

I AM
ENTHUSIASTIC

Being enthusiastic means to hold an
attitude of excitement each and every
day. Be happy and excited about what you
offer to the WORLD with an increased
level of energy towards expectancy!

I AM _____

_____

_____

_____

_____

_____

_____

_____

_____

_____

_____

_____

_____

_____

_____

_____

_____

I AM

"Therefore, if anyone is in Christ, he is a new creation; old things have passed away; behold, all; things have become new."
II Corinthians 5:17 (NKJV)

"Jesus said to them, "Most assuredly, I say to you, before Abraham was, I AM."
John 8:58 (NKJV)

Say It...

I AM EVOLVED

Being evolved is a daily reflection that we aren't the same person we use to be, you are a new creature in Christ, and as a new person we must accept and realize that people hearts, thoughts, and comments matter. We don't have to respond to everything we hear!

I AM _____

_____

_____

_____

_____

_____

_____

_____

_____

_____

_____

_____

_____

_____

_____

_____

_____

_____

I AM

"Keep a cool head. Stay alert. The Devil is poised to pounce, and would like nothing better than to catch you napping. Keep your guard up. You're not the only ones plunged into these hard times. It's the same with Christians all over the world. So keep a firm grip on the faith. The suffering won't last forever. It won't be long before this generous God who has great plans for us in Christ – eternal and glorious plans they are! – will have you put together and on your feet for good. He gets the last word: yes, He does."

1 Peter 5:8-11 (MSG)

Say It...

I AM EFFECTIVE

Being effective is understanding that for every action there is a reaction. And I want to ensure that our lives make a LOUD CAUSE to create a POSITIVE LOUD EFFECT.

I AM _____

_____

_____

_____

_____

_____

_____

_____

_____

_____

_____

_____

_____

_____

_____

_____

I AM

"Jesus was matter-of-fact: "Embrace this God-life. Really embrace it, and nothing will be too much for you. This mountain, for instance: Just say, 'Go jump in the lake'— no shuffling or shilly-shallying—and it's as good as done. That's why I urge you to pray for absolutely everything, ranging from small to large. Include everything as you embrace this God-life, and you'll get God's everything. And when you assume the posture of prayer, remember that it's not all asking. If you have anything against someone, forgive —only then will your heavenly Father be inclined to also wipe your slate clean of sins."

Mark 11:22-25 (MSG)

I AM FORGIVEN

You can rest assured that being forgiven means
God is not concerned with where you fail? He
is more concerned with how you get up and
encourage others, so they can also be forgiven.

I AM

_____

_____

_____

_____

_____

_____

_____

_____

_____

_____

_____

_____

_____

_____

_____

_____

_____

_____

I AM

""God spoke: "Let us make human beings in our image, make them reflecting our nature So they can be responsible for the fish in the sea, the birds in the air, the cattle, And, yes, Earth itself, and every animal that moves on the face of Earth." God created human beings; he created them godlike, Reflecting God's nature. He created them male and female. God blessed them: "Prosper! Reproduce! Fill Earth! Take charge! Be responsible for fish in the sea and birds in the air, for every living thing that moves on the face of Earth." Then God said, "I've given you every sort of seed-bearing plant on Earth And every kind of fruit-bearing tree, given them to you for food. To all animals and all birds, everything that moves and breathes, I give whatever grows out of the ground for food." And there it was. God looked over everything he had made; it was so good, so very good! It was evening, it was morning— Day Six."

Genesis 1:26-31 (MSG)

Say It...

I AM FULFILLED

Being fulfilled is being grateful and content
with what you have now. Its ok to want more.
However, be fulfilled in this very moment.

I AM _____

_____

_____

_____

_____

_____

_____

_____

_____

_____

_____

_____

_____

_____

_____

_____

_____

I AM

"Take good counsel and accept correction—
that's the way to live wisely and well.
We humans keep brainstorming options and
plans, but God's purpose prevails."
Proverbs 19:20-21 (MSG)

Say It...
I AM FLEXIBLE

Being flexible is the willingness to bend, turn, stop, or go when necessary to get anything done. It's okay to take twists and turns on your journey. Flexibility will get you to your destination, not rigidity.

I AM _____

_____

_____

_____

_____

_____

_____

_____

_____

_____

_____

_____

_____

_____

_____

_____

_____

_____

I AM

"Set your minds on things that are above,
not on things that are on Earth."
Colossians 3:2 (ESV)

"But seek first the kingdom of God and his righteousness,
and all these things will be added to you."
Matthew 6:33 (ESV)

Say It...

I AM FOCUSED

Being focused is executing a task or
meeting a goal from start to finish.
Focus requires directing the necessary
energy toward completion.

I AM _____

_____

_____

_____

_____

_____

_____

_____

_____

_____

_____

_____

_____

_____

_____

_____

_____

I AM

"Be strong and courageous. Do not fear or be in dread of them, for it is the Lord your God who goes with you. He will not leave you or forsake you."
Deuteronomy 31:6 (ESV)

Say It...

I AM FEARLESS

You are fearless when you walk towards your fear in faith. You will win no matter what.

I AM

I AM

"Be cheerful no matter what; pray all the time; thank
God no matter what happens. This is the way God
wants you who belong to Christ Jesus to live."
1 Thessalonians 5:16-18 (MSG)

Say It...

I AM GRATITUDE

Gratitude is the state of being thankful for
your life, people, possessions and experiences,
whether they're positive or negative. Afterall,
everything works out for your good.

I AM _____

_____

_____

_____

_____

_____

_____

_____

_____

_____

_____

_____

_____

_____

_____

_____

_____

_____

"Do not lie to one another, seeing that you have
put off the old self with its practices."
Colossians 3:9 (ESV)

Say It...

I AM GENUINE

Be your most authentic self at all times.
Whatever the spirit is moving you to do, do
it without question. If you feel the gumption
to say or do something, walk in your truth.

I AM _____

_____

_____

_____

_____

_____

_____

_____

_____

_____

_____

_____

_____

_____

_____

_____

I AM

"When I was a child, I spoke like a child, I thought like a child, I reasoned like a child. When I became a man, I gave up childish ways."
1 Corinthians 13:11 (ESV)

Say It...

I AM GROWING

Being open to growth means that you
can look back over your life, see how you
have progressed, and celebrate that!

I AM _____

_____

_____

_____

_____

_____

_____

_____

_____

_____

_____

_____

_____

_____

_____

_____

I AM

"Be generous. Give to the poor. Get yourselves a bank that can't go bankrupt, a bank in heaven far from bank robbers, safe from embezzlers, a bank you can bank on. It's obvious, isn't it? The place where your treasure is, is the place you will most want to be, and end up being."

Luke12:33-34 (MSG)

Say It...

I AM GENEROUS

Being generous is the best position anyone can be in. Having a generous hand means your hand is open. Ironically, generosity also positions you to receive.

I AM

"Wise men and women are always learning,
always listening for fresh insights.
A gift gets attention; it buys the attention of eminent people."
Proverbs 18:15-16 (MSG)

I AM GIFTED

Being gifted is realizing that God has given
everyone a measure of talents to live by!
Find and hone your gifts, so they can provide
resources to create income. Sharing your
unique gifts is ultimately living your best life!

I AM _____

_____

_____

_____

_____

_____

_____

_____

_____

_____

_____

_____

_____

_____

_____

_____

I AM

"This is the kind of life you've been invited into, the kind of life Christ lived. He suffered everything that came His way so you would know that it could be done, and also know how to do it, step-by-step. He never did one thing wrong, Not once said anything amiss. They called Him every name in the book and he said nothing back. He suffered in silence, content to let God set things right. He used his servant body to carry our sins to the Cross so we could be rid of sin, free to live the right way. His wounds became your healing. You were lost sheep with no idea who you were or where you were going. Now you're named and kept for good by the Shepherd of your souls."

1 Peter 2:21-25 (MSG)

Say It...

I AM HEALED

Being healed starts within the mind and the spirit. No matter what may be affecting your body, believe you are healed by Faith.

I AM _____

_____

_____

_____

_____

_____

_____

_____

_____

_____

_____

_____

_____

_____

_____

_____

I AM

"A cheerful heart brings a smile to your face;
a sad heart makes it hard to get through the day."
Proverbs 15:13 (MSG)

Say It...

I AM HAPPY

Being happy is a choice that is yours for the choosing every single day. Although sad things may happen, you can find the silver lining. Each person is responsible for their happiness.

I AM _____

_____

_____

_____

_____

_____

_____

_____

_____

_____

_____

_____

_____

_____

_____

_____

_____

_____

I AM

"Or do you not know that your body is a
temple of the Holy Spirit within you,
whom you have from God? You are not your own."
1 Corinthians 6:19 (ESV)

"So, whether you eat or drink, or whatever
you do, do all to the glory of God."
1 Corinthians 10:31 (ESV)

Say It...
I AM HEALTHY

Being healthy is a choice to move your body and fuel your body with good food. Health is also mental and spiritual; fortify your temple by managing your spiritual and mental health with professional guidance.

I AM _____

_____

_____

_____

_____

_____

_____

_____

_____

_____

_____

_____

_____

_____

_____

_____

I AM

"Then Jesus turned to the Jews who had claimed to believe in Him. "If you stick with this, living out what I tell you, you are my disciples for sure. Then you will experience for yourselves the truth, and the truth will free you."

John 8:31-32 (MSG)

Say It...

I AM HONEST

Being honest means telling the truth at any cost. It doesn't matter what people's responses will be. Even if it may get you into "trouble" – honesty always works for your good in the long run.

I AM _____

_____

_____

_____

_____

_____

_____

_____

_____

_____

_____

_____

_____

_____

_____

_____

_____

I AM

"Honor the Lord with your wealth, and with
the first fruits of all your produce."
Proverbs 3:9 (ESV)

"Whoever oppresses a poor man insults his Maker,
but he who is generous to the needy honors him."
Proverbs 14:31 (ESV)

Say It...

I AM HONORABLE

Being honorable is to be above board in all things. How do you live your life when no one is looking? How you live your life when the lights are turned down? How do you live your life when you're alone? To be honorable is to live life with integrity.

I AM _____

_____

_____

_____

_____

_____

_____

_____

_____

_____

_____

_____

_____

_____

_____

_____

_____

I AM

"You are the salt of the earth, but if salt has lost its taste, how shall its saltiness be restored? It is no longer good for anything except to be thrown out and trampled under people's feet. You are the light of the world. A city set on a hill cannot be hidden. Nor do people light a lamp and put it under a basket, but on a stand, and it gives light to all in the house. In the same way, let your light shine before others, so that [a] they may see your good works and give glory to your Father who is in heaven.

Matthew 5:13-16 (ESV)

Say It...

I AM INFLUENTIAL

To be influential is to recognize that people are watching you. Be mindful that young people may imitate you. Understand the power in the fact that you are a living example.

I AM _____

_____

_____

_____

_____

_____

_____

_____

_____

_____

_____

_____

_____

_____

_____

_____

_____

_____

I AM

"He has filled them with skill to do every sort of work done by an engraver or by a designer or by an embroiderer in blue and purple and scarlet yarns and fine twined linen, or by a weaver —by any sort of workman or skilled designer."
Exodus 35:35 (ESV)

Say It...

I AM INNOVATIVE

Being innovative is a reminder that
we are co-creators with Christ. Our
imaginations will spark ideas that can
change the world as we know it.

I AM _____

_____

_____

_____

_____

_____

_____

_____

_____

_____

_____

_____

_____

_____

_____

_____

_____

I AM

"What then shall we say to these things? If God is for us, who can be [a] against us?"

Romans 8:31 (ESV)

Say It...

I AM IMPORTANT

Being important is not being important
in the eyes of men; it's being important
to yourself – and knowing that what you
bring to the world is highly valuable.

I AM _____

_____

_____

_____

_____

_____

_____

_____

_____

_____

_____

_____

_____

_____

_____

_____

I AM

"For I know the plans I have for you," declares the Lord, "plans to prosper you and not to harm you, plans to give you hope and a future."
Jeremiah 29:11 (NIV)

Say It...

I AM INSPIRED

When you witness something that radiates within, go with it. Let it grow into a full fire. Make your why bigger than yourself.

I AM _____

_____

_____

_____

_____

_____

_____

_____

_____

_____

_____

_____

_____

_____

_____

I AM

"Then King Nebuchadnezzar was astonished; and he rose in haste and spoke, saying to his [a]counselors, 'Did we not cast three men bound into the midst of the fire?' They answered and said to the king, 'True, O King.' 'Look!' he answered, "I see four men loose, walking in the midst of the fire; and they are not hurt, and the form of the fourth is like the[b] Son of God."

Daniel 3:24-25 (NKJV)

Say It...

I AM IGNITED

Being ignited means being on fire.
Its allowing someone or something
to excite you to movement.

I AM _____

_____

_____

_____

_____

_____

_____

_____

_____

_____

_____

_____

_____

_____

_____

_____

_____

I AM

"This is the day that the Lord has made;
let us rejoice and be glad in it."

Psalm 118:24 (ESV)

Say It...

I AM JOYOUS

Being joyous is a declaration of your happiness.

I AM _____

_____

_____

_____

_____

_____

_____

_____

_____

_____

_____

_____

_____

_____

_____

_____

_____

_____

I AM

"Don't pick on people, jump on their failures, criticize their faults—unless, of course, you want the same treatment. That critical spirit has a way of boomeranging. It's easy to see a smudge on your neighbor's face and be oblivious to the ugly sneer on your own. Do you have the nerve to say, 'Let me wash your face for you,' when your own face is distorted by contempt? It's this whole traveling road-show mentality all over again, playing a holier-than-thou part instead of just living your part. Wipe that ugly sneer off your own face, and you might be fit to offer a washcloth to your neighbor."

Matthew 7:1-5 (MSG)

Say It...

I AM JUSTIFIED

Being justified is knowing that you are moving in the right direction and being pleasing to God.

I AM _____

_____

_____

_____

_____

_____

_____

_____

_____

_____

_____

_____

_____

_____

_____

_____

_____

I AM

"By faith, we see the world called into existence by God's word, what we see created by what we don't see."
Hebrews 11:3 (MSG)

Say It...

I AM A JET-SETTER

Being a jet-setter means being able
to move about: place to place, city to
city, state to state, country to country,
making the world your own and leaving
each place better than you found it.

I AM _____

_____

_____

_____

_____

_____

_____

_____

_____

_____

_____

_____

_____

_____

_____

_____

_____

I AM

"The heart of the wise makes his speech judicious
and adds persuasiveness to his lips."

Proverbs 16:23 (ESV)

Say It...
I AM JUDICIOUS

Being judicious is utilizing good judgement when opportunities arrive, or choices are presented. You can make clear decisions with emotional intelligence.

I AM _____

_____

_____

_____

_____

_____

_____

_____

_____

_____

_____

_____

_____

_____

_____

_____

_____

I AM

"Bless the Lord, O my soul: and all that is
within me, bless His holy name."
Psalm 103:1 (KJV)

Say It...
I AM JAUNTY
Being jaunty is expressing yourself in a lively
cheerful manner with self-confidence.

I AM _____

_____

_____

_____

_____

_____

_____

_____

_____

_____

_____

_____

_____

_____

_____

_____

_____

I AM

"If I give everything I own to the poor and even go to the stake to be burned as a martyr, but I don't love, I've gotten nowhere. So, no matter what I say, what I believe, and what I do, I'm bankrupt without love. Love never gives up. Love cares more for others than for self. Love doesn't want what it doesn't have. Love doesn't strut, doesn't have a swelled head, doesn't force itself on others, isn't always "me first," doesn't fly off the handle, doesn't keep score of the sins of others, doesn't revel when others grovel, takes pleasure in the flowering of truth, puts up with anything, trusts God always, always looks for the best, never looks back, but keeps going to the end."

1 Corinthians 13:3-7 (MSG)

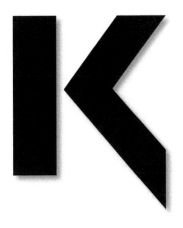

Say It...
I AM KIND

Being kind will get you so far. I can remember just a smile and hello walking down a hallway led me to become Rondell Lancaster in Ambitions. Kindness is free so give it away often.

I AM _____

_____

_____

_____

_____

_____

_____

_____

_____

_____

_____

_____

_____

_____

_____

_____

_____

I AM

"Teach me good judgment and knowledge: for
I have believed thy commandments."
Psalm 119:66 (KJV)

"A wise person is hungry for knowledge,
while the fool feeds on trash."
Proverbs 15:14 (NLT)

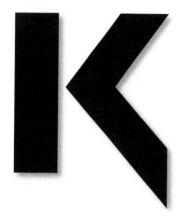

Say It...
I AM
KNOWLEDGEABLE

Being knowledgeable means taking the time to validate, confirm and study a topic for understanding before sharing it.

I AM

_____

_____

_____

_____

_____

_____

_____

_____

_____

_____

_____

_____

_____

_____

I AM

"Keen insight wins favor, but the conduct
of the unfaithful is harsh."
Proverbs 13:15 (NET)

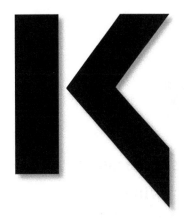

I AM KEEN

Being keen is having the discernment
to make prudent, wise decisions.

I AM _____

_____

_____

_____

_____

_____

_____

_____

_____

_____

_____

_____

_____

_____

_____

_____

I AM

"Let him kiss me with the kisses of his mouth,
for your love is better than wine."

Song of Solomon 1:2 (NKJV)

Say It...

I AM KISSABLE

Being kissable is owning that you are
both worthy and capable of love.

I AM _____

_____

_____

_____

_____

_____

_____

_____

_____

_____

_____

_____

_____

_____

_____

_____

I AM

"She is more precious than jewels,
and nothing you desire can compare with her."
Proverbs 3:15 (ESV)

Say It...

I AM A KEEPER

You are a value to those who connect to your
most authentic self. Know your tribe.

I AM _____

_____

_____

_____

_____

_____

_____

_____

_____

_____

_____

_____

_____

_____

_____

_____

_____

_____

I AM

"For God so loved the world, that he gave His only Son, that whoever believes in him should not perish, but have eternal life."

John 3:16 (ESV)

Say It...
I AM LOVE

Being the embodiment of love proves that you
are a reflection of God, because God is LOVE.

I AM _____

_____
_____
_____
_____
_____
_____
_____
_____
_____
_____
_____
_____
_____
_____
_____
_____
_____
_____

I AM

"Above all, love each other deeply, because love covers over a multitude of sins."

1 Peter 4:8 (NIV)

Say It...
I AM LOVED

Being loved is knowing that someone cares for you unconditionally. Jesus cares for us all.

I AM _____

_____

_____

_____

_____

_____

_____

_____

_____

_____

_____

_____

_____

_____

_____

_____

_____

I AM

"In my Father's house are many mansions: if it were not so,
I would have told you. I go to prepare a place for you."
John 14:2 (KJV)

Say It...

I AM LUXURY

You can have anything you want in this life. You deserve everything you desire because you live in abundance. There is nothing in this life that is withheld from you. You deserve the best of the best.

I AM _____

_____

_____

_____

_____

_____

_____

_____

_____

_____

_____

_____

_____

_____

_____

_____

I AM

"A man of many companions may come to ruin, but there is a friend who sticks closer than a brother."
Proverbs 18:24 (ESV)

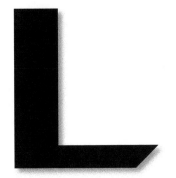

Say It...
I AM LOYAL

Being loyal means that you are
reliable, trustworthy, and give firm
and consistent support to a person or
institution. Loyalty is also allyship that
defends, even when unpopular.

I AM _____

_____

_____

_____

_____

_____

_____

_____

_____

_____

_____

_____

_____

_____

_____

_____

I AM

"And let us not grow weary of doing good, for in due season we will reap, if we do not give up. So then, as we have opportunity, let us do good to everyone, and especially to those who are of the household of faith."
"Do you see a man skillful in his work? He will stand before kings; he will not stand before obscure men."
Proverbs 22:29 (ESV)

Say It...

I AM A LEADER

Being a leader can happen at every level.
Simply lead with a good personality, good
energy, while operating in excellence
and helping others achieve.

I AM _____

_____

_____

_____

_____

_____

_____

_____

_____

_____

_____

_____

_____

_____

_____

I AM

"But he said to me, 'My grace is sufficient for you, for my power is made perfect in weakness.' Therefore. I will boast all the more gladly about my weaknesses, so that Christ's power may rest on me."

2 Corinthians 12:9 (NIV)

Say It...

I AM A MOTIVATED

Being motivated means you put an idea into action. Start now, even if you don't have all the resources. Your motivation is a magnet for success.

I AM _____

_____

_____

_____

_____

_____

_____

_____

_____

_____

_____

_____

_____

_____

_____

_____

_____

I AM

"Oh yes, you shaped me first inside, then out; you formed me in my mother's womb. I thank you, High God —you're breathtaking! Body and soul, I am marvelously made! I worship in adoration—what a creation! You know me inside and out, you know every bone in my body; You know exactly how I was made, bit by bit, how I was sculpted from nothing into something. Like an open book, you watched me grow from conception to birth; all the stages of my life were spread out before you, The days of my life all prepared before I'd even lived one day."

Psalm 139:13-16 (MSG)

I AM A MIRACLE

Being a miracle is that very breath you just took, how your heart is beating right now, and remembering all that you have survived.

I AM _____

_____

_____

_____

_____

_____

_____

_____

_____

_____

_____

_____

_____

_____

_____

I AM

"Don't be misled: No one makes a fool of God. What a person plants, he will harvest. The person who plants selfishness, ignoring the needs of others— ignoring God— harvests a crop of weeds. All he'll have to show for his life is weeds! But the one who plants in response to God, letting God's Spirit do the growth work in him, harvests a crop of real life, eternal life."
Galatians 6:7-8 (MSG)

Say It...

I AM A MILLIONAIRE

Being a millionaire is about so much more than money and having it. It's about the good you can do in the world!

I AM _____

_____

_____

_____

_____

_____

_____

_____

_____

_____

_____

_____

_____

_____

_____

I AM

"But that doesn't mean you should all look and speak and act the same. Out of the generosity of Christ, each of us is given his own gift. The text for this is, He climbed the high mountain, He captured the enemy and seized the booty, He handed it all out in gifts to the people. Is it not true that the One who climbed up also climbed down, down to the valley of Earth? And the One who climbed down is the One who climbed back up, up to highest heaven. He handed out gifts above and below, filled heaven with his gifts, filled Earth with his gifts. He handed out gifts of apostle, prophet, evangelist, and pastor-teacher to train Christ's followers in skilled servant work, working within Christ's body, the church, until we're all moving rhythmically and easily with each other, efficient and graceful in response to God's Son, fully mature adults, fully developed within and without, fully alive like Christ."

Ephesians 4:7-13 (MSG)

Say It...
I AM MAGIC

Being magic is having a unique surprising
element that only you can bring to the world.
Look at your fingerprint, you are MAGIC!

I AM _____

_____

_____

_____

_____

_____

_____

_____

_____

_____

_____

_____

_____

_____

_____

_____

_____

I AM

"Don't fool yourself into thinking that you are a listener when you are anything but, letting the Word go in one ear and out the other. Act on what you hear! Those who hear and don't act are like those who glance in the mirror, walk away, and two minutes later have no idea who they are, what they look like."

James 1:22-24 (MSG)

I AM MAXIMIZING ALL MOMENTS

Leveling up on all your encounters
making sure you're fully present, engaged,
giving and receiving at every level, so
that you and others can benefit.

I AM _____

_____

_____

_____

_____

_____

_____

_____

_____

_____

_____

_____

_____

_____

_____

_____

_____

I AM

"Men and women who have lived wisely and well
will shine brilliantly, like the cloudless, star-strewn
night skies. And those who put others on the right
path to life will glow like stars forever."
Daniel 12:3 (MSG)

I AM NEGOTIATING WISE DEALS

Being a wise negotiator isn't always
about getting the most money;
sometimes wisdom in negotiation means
doing the greatest good for all.

I AM _____

_____

_____

_____

_____

_____

_____

_____

_____

_____

_____

_____

_____

_____

_____

_____

I AM

"But look! A king will rule in the right way,
and his leaders will carry out justice.
Each one will stand as a shelter from high winds, provide safe
cover in stormy weather. Each will be cool running water
in parched land, a huge granite outcrop giving shade in the
desert. Anyone who looks will see, anyone who listens will
hear. The impulsive will make sound decisions, the tongue-
tied will speak with eloquence. No more will fools become
celebrities, nor crooks be rewarded with fame. For fools are
fools and that's that, thinking up new ways to do mischief.
They leave a wake of wrecked lives and lies about GOD, turning
their backs on the homeless hungry, ignoring those dying of
thirst in the streets. And the crooks? Underhanded sneaks they
are, inventive in sin and scandal, Exploiting the poor with
scams and lies, unmoved by the victimized poor. But those
who are noble make noble plans and stand for what is noble."

Isaiah 32:1-8 (MSG)

Say It...
I AM NOBLE

Being noble is having high moral principles and ideals. As you live your life, be concerned with the greatest social and political good.

I AM _____

_____

_____

_____

_____

_____

_____

_____

_____

_____

_____

_____

_____

_____

_____

_____

_____

I AM

"Love the Lord your God with all your heart and with all your soul and with all your mind and with all your strength.' 31 The second is this: 'Love your neighbor as yourself." There is no commandment greater than these."

Mark 12:30-31(NIV)

Say It...

I AM NICE

Be nice regardless of how others treat you, a sweet disposition always wins.

I AM _____

_____

_____

_____

_____

_____

_____

_____

_____

_____

_____

_____

_____

_____

_____

_____

I AM

"Point your kids in the right direction—
when they're old they won't be lost."
Proverbs 22:6 (MSG)

Say It...

I AM NURTURING

To nurture is to contribute to the growth of another, of a project, or a dream on its way to realization. It means being patient, loving, and calming in every situation.

I AM

_____

_____

_____

_____

_____

_____

_____

_____

_____

_____

_____

_____

_____

_____

_____

_____

_____

"So let's not allow ourselves to get fatigued doing good. At the right time we will harvest a good crop if we don't give up or quit. Right now, therefore, every time we get the chance, let us work for the benefit of all, starting with the people closest to us in the community of faith."
Galatians 6:9-10 (MSG)

Say It...

I AM NEVER GIVING UP

Never giving up is being one who will
go the distance to accomplish a task!

I AM _____

_____

_____

_____

_____

_____

_____

_____

_____

_____

_____

_____

_____

_____

_____

I AM

"For it is by grace you have been saved, through faith—and this is not from yourselves, it is the gift of God— not by works, so that no one can boast."
Ephesians 2:8-9 (NIV)

I AM OPTIMISTIC

Being optimistic is seeing the
rainbow in every cloud.

I AM _____

_____

_____

_____

_____

_____

_____

_____

_____

_____

_____

_____

_____

_____

_____

_____

_____

_____

I AM

"All this I have spoken while still with you.
But the Advocate, the Holy Spirit,
whom the Father will send in my name, will teach you
all things and will remind you of everything I have said
to you. Peace I leave with you; my peace I give you.
I do not give to you as the world gives. Do not let
your heart be troubled and do not be afraid.
John 14:25-27 (NIV)

Say It...

I AM OPEN

Being open means being
receptive to all options.

I AM _____

_____

_____

_____

_____

_____

_____

_____

_____

_____

_____

_____

_____

_____

_____

_____

_____

_____

I AM

"Study to shew thyself approved unto God, a workman that needeth not to be ashamed, rightly dividing the word of truth."
2 Timothy 2:15 (KJV)

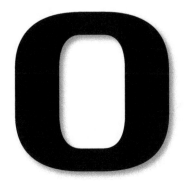

Say It...

I AM OUTSTANDING

Being outstanding is crossing all Ts and dotting all Is – working with excellence in mind!

I AM _____

_____

_____

_____

_____

_____

_____

_____

_____

_____

_____

_____

_____

_____

_____

_____

I AM

"The thief cometh not, but for to steal, and to kill,
and to destroy; I am come that hey might have life,
and that they might have it more abundantly."
John 10:10 (KJV)

Say It...

I AM OPULENT

Being opulent refers to a richness; a luxurious, lavish mindset. Yes, you can enjoy material things, but opulence also conveys to you something valuable that you can offer someone else. Opulence is to be shared.

I AM _____

_____

_____

_____

_____

_____

_____

_____

_____

_____

_____

_____

_____

_____

_____

_____

_____

I AM

"Therefore, I urge you, brothers and sisters, in view of God's mercy, to offer your bodies as a living sacrifice, holy and pleasing to God—this is your true and proper worship. Do not conform to the pattern of this world, but be transformed by the renewing of your mind. Then you will be able to test and approve what God's will is—his good, pleasing and perfect will."
Romans 12:1-2 (NIV)

Say It...

I AM OFFERING MY BEST

Offering my best is when you give your full
attention and resources to something!

I AM _____

_____

_____

_____

_____

_____

_____

_____

_____

_____

_____

_____

_____

_____

_____

_____

I AM

"His master replied, 'Well done, good and faithful servant! You have been faithful with a few things; I will put you in charge of many things. Come and share your master's happiness!'"

Matthew 25:23 (NIV)

Say It...

I AM PROSPEROUS

Being prosperous is claiming that you
live in abundance and everything
you touch is successful – Because you
know you have done the work.

I AM _____

_____

_____

_____

_____

_____

_____

_____

_____

_____

_____

_____

_____

_____

_____

_____

_____

I AM

My dear brothers and sisters, take note of this: everyone should be quick to listen, slow to speak and slow to become angry."

James 1:19 (NIV)

I AM POSITIVE

Being positive is a choice. Negative energy
and destructive self-talk can overwhelm
one's thoughts. Thinking from a positive
place takes intention and practice.

I AM _____

_____

_____

_____

_____

_____

_____

_____

_____

_____

_____

_____

_____

_____

_____

_____

_____

_____

I AM

"I will instruct you and teach you in the way you should go; I will counsel you with my loving eye on you."
Psalm 32:8 (NIV)

Say It...

I AM PASSIONATE

Being passionate is possessing the longing
to do something from deep within, a
place of love that stands in truth.

I AM _____

_____

_____

_____

_____

_____

_____

_____

_____

_____

_____

_____

_____

_____

_____

_____

I AM

"Love is patient, love is kind. It does not envy,
it does not boast, it is not proud.
It does not dishonor others, it is not self-seeking,
it is not easily angered, it keeps no record of wrongs.
1 Corinthians 13:4-5 (NIV)

I AM PATIENT

Being patient is having the ability to slow down when you want things and people to hurry up. It is the practice of humility as miracles take shape.

I AM _____

_____

_____

_____

_____

_____

_____

_____

_____

_____

_____

_____

_____

_____

_____

_____

I AM

"As they left Bethany the next day, he was hungry. Off in
the distance he saw a fig tree in full leaf. He came up to it
expecting to find something for breakfast but found nothing
but fig leaves. (It wasn't yet the season for figs.) He addressed
the tree: 'No one is going to eat fruit from you again—ever!'
And his disciples overheard him.
In the morning, walking along the road, they saw the fig
tree, shriveled to a dry stick. Peter, remembering what
had happened the previous day, said to him, 'Rabbi,
look—the fig tree you cursed is shriveled up!'"
Mark 11:12-14, 20-211 (MSG)

I AM PRODUCTIVE

Productivity isn't just a term for performance
in business. In the Bible, God cursed
the fruitless fig tree. To be productive is
to bear fruit from your tree. Fruit isn't
just pretty on a tree; it is literal produce,
meant to nourish someone else.

I AM _____

_____

_____

_____

_____

_____

_____

_____

_____

_____

_____

_____

_____

_____

_____

_____

_____

I AM

"It will happen in a moment, in the blink of an eye,
when the last trumpet is blown. For when the trumpet
sounds, those who have died will be raised to live forever.
And we who are living will also be transformed."
1 Corinthians 15:52 (NLT)

Say It...

I AM QUICK

Being quick to make a decision is ideal. The faster you can come to a conclusion, the faster you can get to where you are going. That's trusting your gut. When the Holy Spirit is speaking to you, you move on that first thing quickly. You don't take time to mull it over or discourage yourself with what ifs. Follow your first mind!

I AM _____

_____

_____

_____

_____

_____

_____

_____

_____

_____

_____

_____

_____

_____

_____

_____

_____

I AM

"The Lord will fight for you, and you have only to be silent."

Exodus 14:14 (ESV)

Say It...
I AM QUIET

Being quiet is important to hear your daily instructions. Morning meditation is a great place to start your quiet time. In stillness, the word of God rings clearly.

I AM _____

_____

_____

_____

_____

_____

_____

_____

_____

_____

_____

_____

_____

_____

_____

_____

"On the last and greatest day of the festival,
Jesus stood and said in a loud voice,
"Let anyone who is thirsty come to me and drink.
Whoever believes in me, as Scripture has said, rivers
of living water will flow from within them."
John 7:37-38 (NIV)

Say It...

I AM QUENCHED

Being quenched is being satisfied. Having
peace with where you are and what you have.

I AM _____

_____

_____

_____

_____

_____

_____

_____

_____

_____

_____

_____

_____

_____

_____

_____

_____

_____

I AM

"The point is this: whoever sows sparingly will also reap sparingly, and whoever sows bountifully [a] will also reap bountifully. Each one must give as he has decided in his heart, not reluctantly or under compulsion, for God loves a cheerful giver."
2 Corinthians 9:6-7 (ESV)

I AM READY

Being ready acknowledges that
your preparation is complete!

I AM _____

_____

_____

_____

_____

_____

_____

_____

_____

_____

_____

_____

_____

_____

_____

_____

I AM

"So do not fear, for I am with you; do not be dismayed,
for I am your God. I will strengthen you and help you;
I will uphold you with my righteous right hand."
Isaiah 41:10 (NIV)

I AM RELIABLE

Being reliable is an attribute that sets the average from the excellent. Being a person others know they can rely upon in times of need or crisis is favorable to the Lord as we are his arms, legs and feet in the Earth.

I AM _____

_____

_____

_____

_____

_____

_____

_____

_____

_____

_____

_____

_____

_____

_____

_____

_____

_____

I AM

"A devout life does bring wealth, but it's the rich simplicity of being yourself before God. Since we entered the world penniless and will leave it penniless, if we have bread on the table and shoes on our feet, that's enough. But if it's only money these leaders are after, they'll self-destruct in no time. Lust for money brings trouble and nothing but trouble. Going down that path, some lose their footing in the faith completely and live to regret it bitterly ever after. But you, Timothy, man of God: Run for your life from all this. Pursue a righteous life — a life of wonder, faith, love, steadiness, courtesy. Run hard and fast in the faith. Seize the eternal life, the life you were called to, the life you so fervently embraced in the presence of so many witnesses."

1 Timothy 6:6-12 (MSG)

I AM RICH

Claim the richness of your life. Be rich in respect to health, relationships and family; not limited to but also including monetarily.

I AM _____

_____

_____

_____

_____

_____

_____

_____

_____

_____

_____

_____

_____

_____

_____

_____

_____

I AM

"Seize life! Eat bread with gusto, drink wine with a robust heart. Oh yes—God takes pleasure in your pleasure! Dress festively every morning. Don't skimp on colors and scarves. Relish life with the spouse you love. Each and every day of our precarious life. Each day is God's gift. It's all you get in exchange. For the hard work of staying alive. Make the most of each one! Whatever turns up, grab it and do it. And heartily! This is your last and only chance at it, for there's neither work to do nor thoughts to think in the company of the dead, where you're most certainly headed."

Ecclesiastes 9:7-10 (MSG)

I AM RESOURCEFUL

The resourceful take small things and
create greatness and joy from them.
They are invincible in making a way.

I AM _____

_____

_____

_____

_____

_____

_____

_____

_____

_____

_____

_____

_____

_____

_____

_____

_____

_____

_____

I AM

"I'll refresh tired bodies; I'll restore tired souls."
Jeremiah 31:25 (MSG)

I AM REFRESHED

Being refreshed means to see every
morning as an opportunity for renewal;
a new beginning, new mercies, and a
new start has been given to you.

I AM _____

_____

_____

_____

_____

_____

_____

_____

_____

_____

_____

_____

_____

_____

_____

_____

_____

_____

I AM

"Jesus went on to make these comments: 'If you're honest in small things, you'll be honest in big things; If you're a crook in small things, you'll be a crook in big things. If you're not honest in small jobs, who will put you in charge of the store? No worker can serve two bosses: he'll either hate the first and love the second, or adore the first and despise the second. You can't serve both God and the Bank.'"

Luke 16:10-13 (MSG)

Say It...

I AM SUCCESSFUL

Success is defined by winning repeatedly.
Be it big or small acknowledge them
all. Not to be measured against others
but against your personal best.

I AM _____

_____

_____

_____

_____

_____

_____

_____

_____

_____

_____

_____

_____

_____

_____

_____

I AM

"Now God has us where he wants us, with all the time in this world and the next to shower grace and kindness upon us in Christ Jesus. Saving is all his idea, and all His work. All we do is trust Him enough to let Him do it. It's God's gift from start to finish! We don't play the major role. If we did, we'd probably go around bragging that we'd done the whole thing! No, we neither make nor save ourselves. God does both the making and saving. He creates each of us by Christ Jesus to join Him in the work He does, the good work He has gotten ready for us to do, work we had better be doing."

Ephesians 2:7-10 (MSG)

Say It...

I AM SOUGHT-AFTER

Being sought after means people are
looking for you and looking to you.
The special skills you possess that can
solve problems make you an asset.

I AM _____

_____

_____

_____

_____

_____

_____

_____

_____

_____

_____

_____

_____

_____

_____

_____

_____

I AM

"Still, anyone selected out for life has hope, for, as they say, 'A living dog is better than a dead lion.' The living at least know something, even if it's only that they're going to die. But the dead know nothing and get nothing. They're a minus that no one remembers. Their loves, their hates, yes, even their dreams, are long gone. There's not a trace of them left in the affairs of this Earth."
Ecclesiastes 9:4-6 (MSG)

Say It...

I AM A SURVIVOR

Being a survivor means that despite life's mental, physical and emotional challenges, you refuse to accept defeat.

I AM

I AM

"Make the Master proud of you by being good citizens. Respect the authorities, whatever their level; they are God's emissaries for keeping order. It is God's will that by doing good, you might cure the ignorance of the fools who think you're a danger to society. Exercise your freedom by serving God, not by breaking the rules. Treat everyone you meet with dignity. Love your spiritual family. Revere God. Respect the government."
1 Peter 2:13-17 (MSG)

Say It...

I AM SOCIAL

Being social is connecting. No one is born to live on an island. Every person's life impacts others.

I AM _____

_____

_____

_____

_____

_____

_____

_____

_____

_____

_____

_____

_____

_____

_____

_____

_____

I AM

"But you, Israel, are my servant. You're Jacob, my first choice, descendants of my good friend Abraham. I pulled you in from all over the world, called you in from every dark corner of the earth, telling you, 'You're my servant, serving on my side. I've picked you. I haven't dropped you.' Don't panic. I'm with you. There's no need to fear, for I'm your God. I'll give you strength. I'll help you. I'll hold you steady, keep a firm grip on you."

Isaiah 41:8-10 (MSG)

Say It...

I AM STRENGTH

Most of us are stronger than we acknowledge.
As you take inventory of your life you'll see
where strength was exposed many times.

I AM _____

_____

_____

_____

_____

_____

_____

_____

_____

_____

_____

_____

_____

_____

_____

_____

I AM

"Then he said, 'Let me go, for the day has broken.' But Jacob said, 'I will not let you go unless you bless me.'"

Genesis 32:26 (ESV)

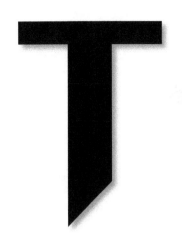

Say It...
I AM TENACIOUS
Tenacity is determination to take
a course of action, to be persistent,
and not easily dispelled.

I AM

Why, even the hairs of your head are all numbered.
Fear not; you are of more value than many sparrows.

Luke 12:7 (ESV)

I AM THOROUGH

Being thorough is staying to the end; seeing
something through to completion.

I AM _____

_____

_____

_____

_____

_____

_____

_____

_____

_____

_____

_____

_____

_____

_____

_____

_____

I AM

"Let the peace of Christ keep you in tune with each other, in step with each other. None of this going off and doing your own thing. And cultivate thankfulness. Let the Word of Christ—the Message—have the run of the house. Give it plenty of room in your lives. Instruct and direct one another using good common sense. And sing, sing your hearts out to God! Let every detail in your lives—words, actions, whatever—be done in the name of the Master, Jesus, thanking God the Father every step of the way."

Colossians 3:15-17 (MSG)

I AM THANKFUL

In all things, give thanks. The power
of gratitude generates positive
energy that creates bounty.

I AM _____

_____

_____

_____

_____

_____

_____

_____

_____

_____

_____

_____

_____

_____

_____

_____

_____

_____

I AM

"Appreciate your pastoral leaders who gave you the Word of God. Take a good look at the way they live, and let their faithfulness instruct you, as well as their truthfulness. There should be a consistency that runs through us all. For Jesus doesn't change— yesterday, today, tomorrow, he's always totally himself."
Hebrews 13:7-8 (MSG)

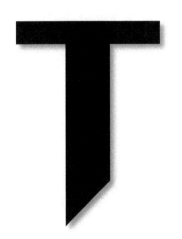

Say It...

I AM TRUSTING

Trust GOD in every circumstance that he is
with you therefore you are never alone.

I AM _____

_____

_____

_____

_____

_____

_____

_____

_____

_____

_____

_____

_____

_____

_____

_____

"Whoever acknowledges me before others,
I will also acknowledge before my Father in heaven."
Matthew 10:32 (NIV)

Say It...

I AM TRANSPARENT

Being transparent is letting people
read the pages of your personal
book from the inside – out.

I AM _____

_____

_____

_____

_____

_____

_____

_____

_____

_____

_____

_____

_____

_____

_____

_____

_____

_____

I AM

"Be wise in the way you act toward outsiders
make the most of every opportunity."
Colossians 4:5 (NIV)

Say It...

I AM UNDERSTANDING

Everyone comes from a different background and unique set of experiences that inform their perceptions and behaviors. This doesn't make them wrong, just different from you. Understanding is the expression of compassion beyond one's own lived experiences.

I AM _____

_____

_____

_____

_____

_____

_____

_____

_____

_____

_____

_____

_____

_____

_____

_____

I AM

"They will be like a tree planted by the water that sends out its roots by the stream. It does not fear when heat comes; its leaves are always green. It has no worries in a year of drought and never fails to bear fruit."
Jeremiah 17:8 (NIV)

Say It...
I AM UNMOVABLE

To be unmovable is to stand firm. Fear cannot sway you. Distractions will not derail you.

I AM _____

_____

_____

_____

_____

_____

_____

_____

_____

_____

_____

_____

_____

_____

_____

_____

_____

_____

I AM

"Even though I walk through the darkest valley,
I will fear no evil, for you are with me; your
rod and your staff, they comfort me."
Psalm 23:4 (NIV)

Say It...

I AM UNBOTHERED

Being unbothered is being steadfast
in the midst of trouble, and
unflappable in the face of drama.

I AM _____

_____

_____

_____

_____

_____

_____

_____

_____

_____

_____

_____

_____

_____

_____

_____

_____

I AM

"You made me; you created me. Now give me the sense to follow your commands. May all who fear you find in me a cause for joy, for I have put my hope in your word."

Psalm 119:73-74 (NLT)

Say It...

I AM UNIQUE

Being unique is leaning into that special way you see the world, hear the world, and move through the world. Your uniqueness is a gift and a blessing.

I AM _____

_____

_____

_____

_____

_____

_____

_____

_____

_____

_____

_____

_____

_____

_____

_____

I AM

"The race is not given to the swift, nor the strong,
but unto them that endure to the end."

Ecclesiastes 9:11 (NIV)

Say It...

I AM UNSTOPPABLE

Absolutely nothing can stop what is for you.
Be relentless in your pursuit of happiness.

I AM _____

_____

_____

_____

_____

_____

_____

_____

_____

_____

_____

_____

_____

_____

_____

_____

_____

I AM

"Make a joyful noise unto the Lord, all ye lands."

Psalm 100 :1 (KJV)

I AM VIVACIOUS

Being vivacious is to exude vitality and effervescence. Putting this kind of energy out into the world yields great returns in every area of one's life – but it starts within, with care for your temple.

I AM _____

_____

_____

_____

_____

_____

_____

_____

_____

_____

_____

_____

_____

_____

_____

_____

_____

_____

I AM

"For the Lord your God is the one who goes with you to fight for you against your enemies to give you victory."
Deuteronomy 20:4 (NIV)

Say It...

I AM VICTORIOUS

Being victorious means even if you lose, you are victorious because you ran your race, your way. You beat your own time. There is no competition.

I AM _____

_____

_____

_____

_____

_____

_____

_____

_____

_____

_____

_____

_____

_____

_____

_____

I AM

"Your vibrant beauty has gotten inside
us - you've been so good to us!
We're walking on air!"
Psalm 89:17 (MSG)

Say It...

I AM VIBRANT

Being vibrant is to be colorful, ever changing, exciting, and filled with passionate energy.

I AM

I AM

"Keep vigilant watch over your heart; that's where
life starts. Don't talk out of both sides of your mouth;
avoid careless banter, white lies, and gossip."

Proverbs 4:23-24 (MSG)

I AM VIGILANT

Being vigilant means to keep watch for possible dangers and difficulties. We know that they are sure to come. We also know that we are already victorious when they arrive.

I AM _____

_____

_____

_____

_____

_____

_____

_____

_____

_____

_____

_____

_____

_____

_____

_____

I AM

"God saw all that he had made, and it was
very good. And there was evening,
and there was morning—the sixth day."
Genesis 1:31 (NIV)

Say It...

I AM VERY GOOD

Being very good is to be content with your
outcome and to commend yourself.

I AM _____

_____

_____

_____

_____

_____

_____

_____

_____

_____

_____

_____

_____

_____

_____

_____

_____

_____

I AM

"Consider it pure joy, my brothers and sisters, [a]
whenever you face trials of many kinds, because you
know that the testing of your faith produces perseverance.
Let perseverance finish its work so that you may be
mature and complete, not lacking anything."
James 1:2-4 (NIV)

Say It...

I AM WISE

Being wise is considering the implications of your decisions. Wisdom is the summation of your knowledge and experiences.

I AM _____

_____

_____

_____

_____

_____

_____

_____

_____

_____

_____

_____

_____

_____

_____

_____

_____

I AM

"Do your very best to present yourself before God as one who
has passed the test – a workman who has no need to be ashamed,
who can carve out a straight path for the word of truth."
2 Timothy 2:15 (NTE)

Say It...

I AM A WINNER

Being a winner is showing up to the competition triumphant before it even starts; it's the attitude that sets you apart.

I AM _____

_____

_____

_____

_____

_____

_____

_____

_____

_____

_____

_____

_____

_____

_____

_____

_____

I AM

"Yet in all these things, we are more than conquerors through Him who loved us."
Romans 8:37 (NKJV)

Say It...

I AM A WARRIOR

Being a warrior facing the giant in your life with boldness and courage. Every warrior has an opponent but the one who is in Christ always has the victory!

I AM _____

_____

_____

_____

_____

_____

_____

_____

_____

_____

_____

_____

_____

_____

_____

_____

_____

"I praise you because I am fearfully and wonderfully made;
your works are wonderful, I know that full well."
Psalm 139:14 (NIV)

Say It...

I AM WONDERFUL

Being wonderful is to celebrate the wonder within, without seeking outside validation.

I AM _____

_____

_____

_____

_____

_____

_____

_____

_____

_____

_____

_____

_____

_____

_____

_____

_____

I AM

Keep on loving one another as brothers and sisters. Do not forget to show hospitality to strangers, for by so doing some people have shown hospitality to angels without knowing it. Continue to remember those in prison as if you were together with them in prison, and those who are mistreated as if you yourselves were suffering.

Hebrews 13:1-3 (NIV)

I AM XENIAL

Being xenial means you are friendly and hospitable, especially to people that you don't know. Be careful how you entertain strangers, it could be an angel.

I AM

_____

_____

_____

_____

_____

_____

_____

_____

_____

_____

_____

_____

_____

_____

_____

I AM

"Beloved, I pray that you may prosper
in all things and be in health,
just as your soul prospers."
3 John 1:2 (NIV)

Say It...

I AM XERARCH

When one is xerarch, it means that one grows and develops, even in dry places. As long as you finish strong, your environment does not dictate your outcome.

I AM _____

_____

_____

_____

_____

_____

_____

_____

_____

_____

_____

_____

_____

_____

_____

_____

_____

I AM

"A good woman is hard to find, and
worth far more than diamonds.
Her husband trusts her without reserve,
and never has reason to regret it.
Never spiteful, she treats him generously all her life long.
She shops around for the best yarns and
cottons, and enjoys knitting and sewing.
She's like a trading ship that sails to faraway places and
brings back exotic surprises. She's up before dawn, preparing
breakfast for her family and organizing her day. She looks over
a field and buys it, then, with money she's put aside, plants a
garden. First thing in the morning, she dresses for work, rolls
up her sleeves, eager to get started. She senses the worth of her
work, is in no hurry to call it quits for the day. She's skilled
in the crafts of home and hearth, diligent in homemaking.
She's quick to assist anyone in need, reaches out to help the
poor. She doesn't worry about her family when it snows; their
winter clothes are all mended and ready to wear. She makes
her own clothing, and dresses in colorful linens and silks.

Her husband is greatly respected when he
deliberates with the city fathers.

She designs gowns and sells them, brings the sweaters she knits
to the dress shops. Her clothes are well-made and elegant, and
she always faces tomorrow with a smile. When she speaks she
has something worthwhile to say, and she always says it kindly.
She keeps an eye on everyone in her household, and keeps
them all busy and productive. Her children respect and bless
her; her husband joins in with words of praise: "Many women
have done wonderful things, but you've outclassed them all!"
"Charm can mislead and beauty soon fades. The woman to be
admired and praised is the woman who lives in the Fear-of-God.
Give her everything she deserves! Festoon her life with praises!"

Proverbs 31:10-31 (MSG)

I AM

What's your favorite scripture?

I AM XENAS

Being Xenas describes women like
Xena, the Warrior Princess and Jael
in the Bible...look them up!

I AM _____

_____

_____

_____

_____

_____

_____

_____

_____

_____

_____

_____

_____

_____

_____

_____

_____

_____

I AM

"The Lord is my Shepard, I lack nothing. He makes me lie down in green pastures, he leads me besides quite waters, he refreshes my soul. He guides me along the right paths for his name's sake."

Psalm 23:1-3 (NIV)

I AM XENAGOGUE

When one is a Xenagogue, they are a guide.
As long as you allow your light to shine, you
will help guide others to their purpose.

I AM _____

_____

_____

_____

_____

_____

_____

_____

_____

_____

_____

_____

_____

_____

_____

_____

_____

_____

"When he was at a table with them, he took the bread and blessed and broke it and gave it to them."

Psalm 23:1-3 (NIV)

Say It...

I AM XENISMOS

Being xenismos is to not only feed GODs people
with food but feed them with the word of GOD.

I AM _____

_____

_____

_____

_____

_____

_____

_____

_____

_____

_____

_____

_____

_____

_____

_____

_____

_____

I AM

"Delight yourself also in the LORD,
and He shall give you the desires of your heart."
Psalm 37:4 (NIV)

I AM YEARNING

Yearning is the intense desire to
have a thing. It causes you to eagerly
and actively work toward obtain it
without stopping until its yours.

I AM _____

_____

_____

_____

_____

_____

_____

_____

_____

_____

_____

_____

_____

_____

_____

_____

_____

_____

I AM

"Love God, all you saints; God takes care of all who stay close to him, but he pays back in full those arrogant enough to go it alone. Be brave. Be strong. Don't give up. Expect God to get here soon."
Psalm 31:19-24 (MSG)

I AM YARE

Being yare is to be malleable, quick and
lively and ready for change without
resistance. Like water; it flows.

I AM _____

_____

_____

_____

_____

_____

_____

_____

_____

_____

_____

_____

_____

_____

_____

_____

I AM

"But Jesus said, 'Let the children come to
me, and don't try to stop them!
People who are like these children belong to God's kingdom.'"
Matthew 19:14 (NIV)

I AM YOUTHFUL

Being youthful is a state of mind: being fun
and vigorous. Being child-like is a superpower.

I AM _____

_____

_____

_____

_____

_____

_____

_____

_____

_____

_____

_____

_____

_____

_____

_____

_____

I AM

"Submit yourselves therefore to God. Resist
the devil, and he will from you.'"

James 4:7 (ESV)

I AM YIELDING

To Yield is to let go of yourself
be fully engulfed in the words
and the ways of the LORD.

I AM _____

_____

_____

_____

_____

_____

_____

_____

_____

_____

_____

_____

_____

_____

_____

_____

_____

_____

I AM

"And I heard the voice of the Lord saying, "Whom shall I send, and who will go for us?" Then I said, "Here I am! Send me.".""
Isaiah 6:8 (ESV)

Say It...

I AM YES

The power of Yes is knowing when to say no.

I AM _____

_____

_____

_____

_____

_____

_____

_____

_____

_____

_____

_____

_____

_____

_____

_____

_____

I AM

And he said: "Truly I tell you, unless you
change and become like little children,
you will never enter the kingdom of heaven.
Matthew 18:3 (NIV)

I AM ZIPPY

To be zippy simply means to be lively,
bright, alert, fresh, and expedient.

I AM _____

_____

_____

_____

_____

_____

_____

_____

_____

_____

_____

_____

_____

_____

_____

_____

_____

I AM

"Don't burn out; keep yourselves fueled and aflame.
Be alert servants of the Master, cheerfully expectant.
Don't quit in hard times; pray all the harder.
Help needy Christians; be inventive in hospitality."
Romans 12:11-13 (MSG)

Say It...

I AM ZEALOUS

Being zealous means to be fervid, fiery, devoted, and passionate about the things you want to accomplish in life.

I AM
_____

_____

_____

_____

_____

_____

_____

_____

_____

_____

_____

_____

_____

_____

_____

_____

_____

_____

I AM

"You are the salt of the earth. But what
good is salt if it has lost its flavor?
Can you make it salty again? It will be thrown
out and trampled underfoot as worthless."
Matthew 5:13-16 (NIV)

I AM ZESTY

To be zesty is to be full of flavor! People
can steal your recipe, but they will
never duplicate your savory taste!

I AM _____

_____

_____

_____

_____

_____

_____

_____

_____

_____

_____

_____

_____

_____

_____

_____

_____

I AM

"Yea, though I walk through the valley of the
shadow of death, I will fear no evil:
for thou art with me; thy rod and thy staff they comfort me."
Psalm 23:4 (NIV)

Say It...

I AM ZEN

Being Zen is emphasizing the value of
meditation and intuition. Find your peace
with stillness and silence as a daily practice.
Start with 2 mins.

I AM _____

_____

_____

_____

_____

_____

_____

_____

_____

_____

_____

_____

_____

_____

_____

_____

_____

_____

I AM

"How beautiful are your feet in sandals, O noble daughter!
Your rounded thighs are like jewels, the work of a master hand.
Your navel is a rounded bowl that never lacks mixed wine.
Your belly is a heap of wheat, encircled with lilies.
Your two breasts are like two fawns, twins of a gazelle.
Your neck is like an ivory tower, Your eyes are pools in Heshbon,
by the gate of Bath-rabbim.Your nose is like a tower of Lebanon,
which looks toward Damascus. Your
head crowns you like Carmel,
and your flowing locks are like purple; a
king is held captive in the tresses.
How beautiful and pleasant you are, O
loved one, with all your delights![a]
Your stature is like a palm tree, and your
breasts are like its clusters.
I say I will climb the palm tree and lay hold of its fruit.
Oh may your breasts be like clusters of the vine, and the scent of
your breath like apples, and your mouth[b] like the best wine.
It goes down smoothly for my beloved,
gliding over lips and teeth.[c]

I am my beloved's, and his desire is for me. Come, my beloved,

let us go out into the fields and lodge in the villages;[d]

let us go out early to the vineyards and see

whether the vines have budded,

whether the grape blossoms have opened and the pomegranates

are in bloom. There I will give you my love. The mandrakes give

forth fragrance, and beside our doors are all choice fruits, new

as well as old, which I have laid up for you, O my beloved."

Song of Solomon 7:1-13 (ESV)

I AM

What's your favorite scripture?

Say It...

I AM ZAFTIG

Being Zaftig is having a shapely and
full figure; voluptuous; full-bosomed.
Whatever your shape is, CELEBRATE it.

I AM

Printed in the USA
CPSIA information can be obtained
at www.ICGtesting.com
LVHW080236160424
777471LV00006B/528